Table of Contents

I. While watching the news one night
II. What is Bully Proof Nation all about
III. What is Bullying
IV. It's an Epidemic
V. Alarming Stats, the Facts.
VI. What can be considered Bullying? STIPE
VII. Bullied boy dies after being beaten by classmates
VIII. Characteristics of the Bully & the Bullied
IX. WIT4LIFE: Solution to Bullying

Introduction

WHILE WATCHING THE NEWS ONE NIGHT

While watching the news one night, sitting on the coach with my wife, my heart went out to a young man that was bullied by two other young men, in which he later attempted to commit suicide. Immediately, it made me furious and upset to hear what was going on in our city of Lexington, Ky. This of course was nothing new, especially to those of big urban cities, it's just that some have coined the phrase to attack the issue at hand in a different approach and to make it a nationwide campaign to fight this problem. Of course I've heard of kids being bullied and even experienced being bullied in school myself, who hasn't. Anyway, this particular night watching the TV was much different. I immediately said to myself what can I do to make a difference in the community this is going on in, and how can I help perhaps help save someone who was being abused, taken advantage of or even bring more awareness to this demeaning action that is effecting many children, and youth in our schools systems and community.

Suddenly, this became a burden to me and as I began doing the research about bullying, it was then that I discovered that bullying was in fact a Nation Wide Epidemic. The stats spoke for themselves, and they were alarming. I will later get into the stats soon, but right now I will focus on sharing with you how this mission to save the innocent from bullies, educated others on bullying, to provide solutions, and to importantly heighten the awareness of bullying. So, thus I began the journey to bring more awareness to bullying but also to provide solutions such as, walking away, taking a deep breath, etc. As I thought about these global steps it was evident that I had a solution right in my hands in the book that I had written two years ago called WIT4Life. I will share some of those behavior modification techniques I have used for over ten years with children and youth for anger management & conflict resolution as a clinical therapist for ten years. My aim is to fight this epidemic with the means that I already possess and to make a difference.

What is Bully Proof Nation All About?

BPN is about bringing to light an epidemic that not only effects one person, but effects a nation, thus having a burden to help provide simple solutions and proven techniques that can help both the bully & the bullied, while providing simple solution & techniques that can be used today for the child, youth parent, and professionals help the child today. You will find in this book a 6 Step process that can help with not only bullying, but also anger management, conflict resolution, ADHD & oppositional defiance in which the author JW Rhodes used for over ten years as a clinical therapist for children and families. That technique is from his book "WIT4LIFE – Anger Management & Conflict Resolution for Children & Youth. He has combined the parts of that book and parts of Bully Proof Nation to provide quick techniques that can be used TODAY! INSTEAD OF WAITING TIL YOU WORD THE WHOLE BOOK. This book is the 2nd of other character building curriculums Coach JW Rhodes has developed over the years to help develop not only the character, but artistic growth in children & youth.

This book BPN is a Bully Proof Nation Guide for students, parents, teachers & youth workers & professionals, that can be applied immediately and with effectiveness, when applied correctly.

Bully Proof Nation Action Plan: R.A.I.D.

Radar: Who do you know that has been a victim of bullying?_____

Action: What are you doing to help the victim?

_____

Insight: We all need someone to look out for us, who are you looking out for?

_____

Diligence: Keeping alert and on guard of bullying helps us to form a defense & offence against bullying

WHAT IS A BULLY?

A Bully, is one who hurts or intimidates weaker or smaller people, according to webster's dictionary.

However, we have found that there are people of small stature that bully those who are bigger than themselves, due to their abrasive & aggressive behavior. I can recall for myself a bully who would try to bully me often, in junior high at Lower Upper Grade Center located on the south side of Chicago. He was no taller than myself, but he was rough and into selling drugs during that time. And yes, we got into a couple of fights, because I had to defend myself, and prove to him that I was not afraid, even though I was to some extent. But I do recall that after the fight I gain respect from him at that point. It's unfortunate that one has to physically fight the bully before they get the picture, "that you are not afraid of them" and of course to protect yourself.

A bully is one who seeks to belittle or gain control over another person in order that they may have advantage point of authority. Bullies come in all types of shapes, sizes, colors and ages. Bullies don't discriminate who they pick on if you have something they want they will waste no time to get it, or if you hold a particular position in statue, power, confidence, the bully will go for it. Again, the bully of today is dressed differently in the since of there make up, but there are ways you can spot the typical bully. They are the ones who get's satisfaction at bringing others down, they get pleasure out of seeing some ones else's pain, the bully of today is narcissistic, only concerned with themselves and very much in love with themselves. They are not the slow academic kid, but they are the ones who yes are very intelligent and knows who doesn't love themselves. Or shall I say they know the ones who have low self esteem so the play on their emotions in order to control or steer them in the direction they so desire. Bullies are not only in school but they are in the work place, but we won't go there today. By the way those childhood bullies end up being adult bullies as well. Anyway, bullies are found almost anywhere, anytime, and in any form shape size or color. Bullies are not always easy to spot they, they sometimes hang out in groups, on-line, in silence waiting on the right time to attack. Often, times the bully will attack when no one is looking. You don't believe me watch the known bully and see when he/she preys upon the victim. Again, we will get into the psychological aspects of a bully later, to discover how and why they display this type of behavior. My aim is to bring light to what a bully is and how bullies operate. We must not stand around in shadow blindness merely saying that we are fully aware but treating the problem as though it's not there and saying it's not truly a real problem, or disregarding it as though it doesn't exist in our own school, by turning a blind eye. We must address bullying as it is and hit the Bull's Eye, that is the solution of the target to this issue.

Bully Proof Nation Action Plan: R.A.I.D.

Radar: Who do you know that has been a victim of bullying?_____

Action: What are you doing to help the victim?

_____

Insight: We all need someone to look out for us, who are you looking out for?

_____

Diligence: Keeping alert and on guard of bullying helps us to form a defense & offence against bullying

It's an Epidemic

Alarming Stats of this epidemic of emotion & physical control

The word Epidemic is defined by webster's, as affecting many people at the same time, it is wide spread, it is a contagious disease."

Stats: Bullying Statistics
- 1 out of 4 teens are Bullied.
- As many as 160,000 students stay home on any given day because they're afraid of being bullied.
- 1 out of 5 kids admits to being a bully, or doing some "Bullying."
- 43% fear harassment in the bathroom at school.
- 282,000 students are physically attacked in secondary schools each month.

More youth violence occurs on school grounds as opposed to on the way to school.

- 80% of the time, an argument with a bully will end up in a physical fight.

- 1/3 of students surveyed said they heard another student threaten to kill someone.

- Playground statistics - Every 7 minutes a child is bullied. Adult intervention 4% Peer intervention 11%.

No intervention - 85%

Right here in lexington,

Sep 5, 2012 ... A man has been arrested in connection to an extreme case of bullying that police say led a teenager to attempt suicide.

<u>Arrest Made In</u> Bullying <u>Case - ABC36 News WTVQ - Wtvq.com</u>: **this incident is what led me to speak out on Bullying, to give solutions against bullying,**

to decrease & and to bring a holt to it and to tell this Big Enemy TO PUT IT AWAY THE HARRASSMENT! TO INTIMIDATION!

Don't Ever Allow the Big Bully to win, by you trying to take your life in attempting suicide.

The question was asked had bullying always been around or our eyes, just simply been close and our emotions totally oblivious to our surrounds. The truth of the matter is that bullying has been around since the beginning of times. Let's take a look at David and Goliath, in which Goliath attempted to use his brute force and statute in order to first of all intimidate the Israelites. But despite it all David knew who's he was, who he was in himself. Which leads me to a very valid point when it comes to standing up for yourself and taking a stand against one who is known as arrogant, boastful, un-defeatable, and undeniably brute and strong, who does the bully pray against most times? He prays against those who may see themselves as a feeble and weak.

MY burden is to seek to protect the feeble and the weak as much as I can and as much territory given & with the authority within my reach, to make sure innocent children are not taken advantage of.

Alarming FACTS & STATS ABOUT BULLYING:

52% of Teens feel the need to try and fit in.

It's important for a teen to be able to connect with someone.

2 Out of 5 Teens feel alone.

Many teens who lack self esteem look to others for self worth

Bully Proof Nation Action Plan: R.A.I.D.

Radar: How will you bring more awareness to this epidemic?_____

Action: What are you doing personally to help decrease bullying?

_____

Insight: We all need someone to look out for us, who are you looking out for?

_____

Diligence: Keeping alert and on guard of bullying helps us to form a defense & offence against bullying

What can be considered Bullying? STIPE

1. Spreading Rumors is a Form of Bullying
2. Intimidation is a Form of Bullying
3. Teasing can be a Form of Bullying
4. Physical Attacks is Bullying
5. Excluding is Bullying

Some after effects of bullying

1. Bullying causes anxiety

2. Bullying causes anger

In some rare and tragic cases, bullying can lead a student that is being bullied into rage and intense anger and cause them to want to get revenge upon peers for bullying.

As a bystander, which is one sees the act of bullying, if you don't speak up or take some action concerning the situation you are sending a message to the bully that it's ok, and to the bullied you don't care what happens to them. You disarm the bully when you stand up to them and the more that can present a united front the better.

However, this united front should be used with some caution so you all will not look as though you are bullying the bully, or ganging up on them.

Reaching out to the bullied

"Recent bullying statistics show that bullying is on the rise among young adults, teens and children. The rise in these bullying statistics is likely due to a fairly recent form of bullying seen in recent years called cyber bullying. This type of bullying has gotten immense media attention over the past few years sighting instances of cyber bullying pushed too far, and in many cases leading to cases of teen suicide or death. Many bullying statistics and studies have found that physical assaults have been replaced with constant cyber assaults in the form of bashing, rumors and other hazing content targeted at a single student or group of students."

Bullying statistics:

- About 42 percent of kids have been bullied while online with one in four being verbally attacked more than once.
- About 35 percent of kids have been threatened online.
- About 58 percent of kids and teens have reported that something mean has been said about them or to them online.
- Other bullying statistics show that about 77 percent of students have admitted to being the victim of one type of bullying or another.
- The American Justice Department bullying statistics show that one out of ever 4 kids will be bullied sometime throughout their adolescence.
- 46 percent of males followed by 26 percent of females have admitted to being victims in physical fights as reported in one report of bullying statistics by the Bureau of Justice School.

Other bullying facts:

- As these bullying statistics indicate, bullying is just getting worse in American schools. Many studies have shown that increasing domestic violence at home are leading to an increase in bullying online and at school.
- Researchers note that one way to help begin to lower these bullying statistics is to tell an adult when it is happening.
- According to the i-Safe American survey of students bullying statistics, about 58 percent of kids admit to never telling an adult when they've been the victim of a bullying attack.
- Another way to stay safe from bullies is to inform the school if the attacks are taking place on school property or have something to do with the school.
- Ignore messages sent by cyber bullies.

Based on the bullying statistics we found, it is clear that cyber bullying is on the rise more so than any other type of bullying. Many students report seeing these types of bullying in chat rooms, social networking websites like MySpace.com and Facebook.com. There has also been websites dedicated to targeting a student or group of students. Many bullying studies revealed that students who are part of a minority group of students based on their gender, race, socioeconomic status as well as sexual preference are reasons other students use to harass and cyber bully one another. Many of these students are forced to deal with at-school bullying and have it follow them home as they see hurtful comments and rumors being said about them throughout the Internet. While this isn't always a school-related issue, many schools are cutting down on this type of behavior from occurring at school by limiting computer time and prohibiting many of the social websites used to spread the hurtful information.

Because of the wide-spread amount of bullying it is more important than ever for parents and teachers to check in with children about bullying. Many students might be afraid to tell an adult or parent, which is why parents and teachers need to be aware of the signs of bullying and to pay attention to what is going on with their child or student. Another one of the best ways to handle bullying to help lower these numbers reported in bullying statistics is open communication. Students and children should be encouraged to tell a trusted adult, parent or teacher about any kind of bullying attack. It is the best way to help stop the situation from getting worse and to help prevent bullying from targeting more and more victims.

Sources: http://www.isafe.org

Bullied boy dies after being beaten by classmates

http://pix11.com/2013/03/04/bullied-boy-dies-after-being-beaten-by-classmates/#axzz2NLUsW4mB

A bullied boy from Philadelphia has died after a brutal attack by two classmates left him in a medically-induced coma.

Bailey O'Neill, who turned 12 on Saturday, died Sunday morning and was taken off life support. Two other pupils jumped Bailey during recess at their Darby Township School, hitting him in the face repeatedly, the boy's father Rob O'Neill told WPVI.

Family of Bailey O'Neill say he was attacked during recess by two classmates at Darby Township School. (NBC Philadelphia)

He suffered a broken nose, a concussion and his personality changed after the attack. "He was sleeping. He was moody.

He wasn't himself. He was angry a little bit. He wasn't really eating," Rob O'Neill told WPVI in February.

His condition worsened over the next couple weeks and was ultimately hospitalized in Wilmington, Delaware after he began vomiting and having seizures. Doctors hoped

placing him in a coma would end the seizures, but they continued. Bailey developed pneumonia and required a blood transfusion.

Bailey O'Neill died after a bullying attack by his own classmates left him in a medically-induced coma. (Facebook)

News of the bully attack spread quickly over the Internet with thousands liking the "Prayers for Bailey O'Neill" Facebook Page. An anti-bullying Pennsylvania House bill has even been created, with nearly a thousand signatures so far.

Baltimore Ravens Star running back Ray Rice is urging parents, teachers and elected officials to act to prevent bullying.

News of Bailey's death inspired Baltimore Ravens star running back Ray Rice to speak out against bullying on Facebook, writing: "After learning last Thursday that doctors said Bailey had no longer had any brain activity, I reached out to the family and was able to spend about 45 minutes on the phone with them. I could hear their sadness, worry, frustration and grief. They would be faced with removing their son, cousin, nephew, and best friend from life support.

I don't think I will ever be able to understand why kids bully each other and how we are all sitting here after yet another "bully death" getting ready to go through this difficult task of picking up the pieces and the even more difficult task of forgiving so we can heal."

Read more at http://pix11.com/2013/03/04/bullied-boy-dies-after-being-beaten-by-classmates/#4kewmiX7DfcLapuK.99

Read more: http://pix11.com/2013/03/04/bullied-boy-dies-after-being-beaten-by-classmates/#ixzz2NLZH1lxK

Characteristics of the Bully & the Bullied:

A Bully Often

- Seeks to dominate and/or manipulate others.
- Enjoys feeling powerful and in control (whether real or not).
- Is both a poor winner (boastful and arrogant) and a poor loser.
- Seems to derive satisfaction from other's fears, discomfort or pain.
- Is good at hiding behaviors or doing them where those in authority can't notice
- Is excited by conflicts between others.
- Blames others for his/her problems.
- Displays uncontrolled anger (rage).
- May have a history of discipline problems.
- Displays a pattern of impulsive and aggressive behaviors.
- Displays intolerance

- May use drugs, alcohol or be recovering from the consumption/withdrawal

- Lacks empathy towards others

Someone Being Bullied Often

- Withdraws socially; has few or no friends.

- Feels isolated, alone and sad.

- Feels picked on or persecuted.

- Feels rejected and not liked.

- Frequently complains of illness.

- Doesn't want to go to work or school

- Displays mood swings and talks

    about hopelessness.

- Talks about leaving; talks of suicide.

- Threatens violence to self and others.

- Changes in eating or sleeping patterns.

- May takes, or attempt to take, "protection" to work or school

- Displays "victim" body language—hangs head,

What Can A Person Do?

- Leave your emotions at the door.

- State your position respectfully, factually.

- Do not take a bully's behavior personally.

- Try to clarify what the other is really saying by using mirroring.

- Make no assumptions.

- Ask questions and stay calm until you understand.

- Build trust by agreeing with the other.

- Alert the other to any problem you foresee.

- Do your homework and be well prepared before you talk.

- If the other has lost self control, politely excuse yourself to go to the bathroom so he/she can calm down.

- Agree to do what the person is asking if not illegal or unethical.

Bully Proof Nation Action Plan: R.A.I.D.

Radar: Who do you know that has been a victim of bullying?_____

Action: What are you doing to help the victim?

_____

Insight: We all need someone to look out for us, who are you looking out for?

_____

Diligence: Keeping alert and on guard of bullying helps us to form a defense & offence against bullying

The Types of Bullying

There are many types of bullying and I have selected 5 types of bullying to write about in this book. Among the types of bullying are:

1. Verbal
2. Social
3. Physical
4. Racial
5. Cyber

Verbal Bullying

The first type of bullying we will examine is verbal bullying. It happens frequently and can happen discretely that those in authority may not notice when the bully is victimizing another or will not catch when it is being done.

Here are some ways to recognize verbal bullying:

- Insulting remarks & put-downs
- Gossiping
- Teasing repeatedly and often
- Name-calling
- Threats and intimidation
- Racist remarks or other harassment
- Whispering behind someone's back

Verbal means using words, auditory. So Verbal bullying can be kinds of name calling, talking about how someone looks or sounds, gossiping, spoken abuse and basically talking about people behind their back, to their face and even attempting to intimate someone, or an attempt to belittle them (so feel smaller then them). The

Department of Education and Early Childhood Development's Building Respectful and Safe Schools (2010) identifies four types of bullying. They say this about verbal bullying, that it includes name calling, insults, teasing, intimidation, homophobic or racist remarks, or verbal abuse. http://www.ncab.org.au/fourkindsofbullying/ .

Social Bullying

Social also called covert bullying assist to harm a person's social reputation and/or cause humiliation, and embarrassment.

NCAB gives ways to recognize Social/Covert bullying which includes:

- lying and spreading rumors
- negative facial or physical gestures, menacing or contemptuous looks
- playing nasty jokes to embarrass and humiliate
- mimicking unkindly
- encouraging others to socially exclude someone
- damaging someone's social reputation or social acceptance. (according to NCAB)

The Aim of the Social Bully is to make you feel like an outsider and to make you feel ostracized, like you don't belong. It is bullies attempt to belittle you and make you feel smaller than life and to crush your self esteem, but don't give the bully them low and to break your spirit. That's right the bully wants to break your sprit but don't allow them to do that. You must be strong and find the help to make sure your life is not compromised in order that another can feel good. You have been placed here on earth and created to make a difference in the world of others, and if you are not feeling good about yourself how can you possibly impact other peoples lives, let alone be productive with your own life. If there is a group of people who don't want you with them, so what, there are plenty of other

groups or people who would welcome you. Besides if they don't want you in their group why be apart of a group that doesn't respect you any way, move on. Lastly, in regards to social exceptence appreciate who you are and don't give some one else the time or the day that can't appreciate who you are, and don't even give them the thoughts in your mind, don't let them take up space, keep your peace and move on. When the bully takes up time in your mind in thought they are winning, so don't let them win, and quickly move on, it hurts them more when they see that it doesn't affect you one bit.

Physical Bullying

What is Physical Bullying?

Bullying, again is one who hurts another repeatedly for gain of power and control.

"Physical bullying occurs when a person uses overt bodily acts to gain power over peers. Physical bullying can include kicking, punching, hitting or other physical attacks.

Unlike other types of bullying in schools, physical bullying is easy to identify because the acts are so obvious. Physical bullies tend to demonstrate high levels of aggression from a young age and are more likely to be boys." From Tween Parenting at http://tweenparenting.about.com/od/socialdevelopment/a/physical-bullying.htm

Bully Proof Nation Action Plan: R.A.I.D.

Radar: Who do you know that has been a victim of physical bullying?_____

Action: What are you doing to help the victim?

_____ What are you doing directly or indirectly to discourage or deter the bully from bullying the victim?_____

Insight: Bullies use physical force to gain control and to dominate over the victim, because they lack the ability to control the verbally.

_____

Diligence: Keeping alert and on guard of ways to help the bully arm themselves through adult intervention or strategic assistance.

Racial Bullying

What is Racist Bullying?

My definition of racial bullying is being abusive towards and controlling over someone because of their skin color, race, culture, or ethic background.

In Kids Scape of www.kidscape.org they have listed how this type of bullying can be recognized.

Kidscape say's Racial Bullying can include:

- physical, verbal or emotional bullying
- insulting or degrading comments, name calling, gestures, taunts, insults or 'jokes'
- offensive graffiti
- humiliating, excluding, tormenting, ridiculing or threatening
- making fun of the customs, music, accent or dress of anyone from a different culture
- refusal to work with or co-operate with others because they are from a different culture

The race relations act 1976 states that schools and governing bodies have a duty to ensure that students do not face any form of racial discrimination, including attacks and harassment.

Kidscape says that there are no easy answers, but providing some helping suggestions on how to handle racial bullying such as:

1. Telling kids on the first day of school that bullying of any kind won't be tolerated.

2. Surveying pupils to find out if they feel it is a problem.

3. Inform parents that they their school is committed to carrying out racial harmony amongst its pupils, staff and the community.

4. Providing educational material on this subject matter to ensure kids, staff, and parents know how to deal with this issue when ever it arise.

I feel also that this is a preventative measure that will help to counter attack the issue, before it grows. As the quote goes, "An once of prevention, is greater than a pound of cure." I am all for preventing matters before they even start if at all possible. Of course in a perfect world this is possible, so we must take extra measures to ensure that this doesn't occur or get out of control, it must be "nipped in the bud" immediately. This is one of the primary reasons that Bully Proof Nation was written. www.bullyproofanation.com

To continue to help pupils & staff learn the efficient and appropriate ways to deal with bullying these needed steps are important:

- Educate & cover prejudice, direct/indirect discrimination, defuse stereotypes, appreciate & celebrating diversity
- Follow guidelines that state that all pupils are entitled to feel safe, secure and respect
- Appreciate the values of people from all cultural, ethnic and religious backgrounds
- Crucial steps of action to educate staff and other officials in government should be trained on equality issues, working with parents, supporting victims, on changing disrespectful & negative behavior and school procedures for resolving bullying

Cyber

What is Cyber Bullying?

Cyber Bullying is the use of the Internet and related technologies for the soul purpose of hurting others, in a hostile, terroristic, deliberately, repeatedly, in a hostile manner. This has become a more common challenge and epidemic in society, especially among our young people. Legislation and statewide legislative awareness campaigns have arisen to combat this huge issue.

In Prevention for Teens | End to Cyber Bullying Organization (ETCB) at http://www.endcyberbullying.org/prevention/prevention-for-teens/

They mention Cyber bullying is can be continuous regardless of whether the target is online. For example, a bully can put very disrespectful comments o remarks on a social media site and it stays there indefinitely. This is how the treatment continues because more and more people find out about and then possible questioning arise and is repetitive and which becomes perpetual humiliation.

Cyber Bullying takes on many forms among the few are:
- Email threats
- Instant messaging chats
- Cell phone messages
- Website with derogatory slants defaming others
- Hacking others screen names and pretending to be someone else
- Forwarding false private messages, pictures, or video to others.

Love Our Children
http://loveourchildrenusa.org/parent_cyberbullying.php
Cyber Bullying is a crime. It's also a crime to publish something that is "libelous" - meaning writing something insulting or something that could harm someone's reputation.

Top 10 Tips on Preventing Cyber Bullying | Computer Tips
http://tips4pc.com/computer_tips_and_tricks/top-10-tips-on-preventing-cyber-bullying.htm

BPN Action Plan: R.A.I.D.

Radar: Who do you know that has been a victim of racial bullying?_____

Action: What are you doing indirectly or directly to help the victim & educate the bully of its effects upon one?

_____

Insight: Rather we chose to believe it or not, when one is looking upon another as though they are lower then you, you have a strong tendency to racially bully another directly or indirectly, even with you pious looks or arrogance.

_____

Diligence: How think about another person eventually comes out in our actions, therefore guard your thoughts about other that are of a different ethnic group.

Bullying happens when individuals intentionally hurt or threaten someone through verbal, physical, or mental abuse. The myth of bullying is that it's a bigger boy pushing around a smaller boy. The reality is bullying happens in many different ways and is instigated by both boys and girls.

Bullying can happen anywhere. Typically bullying tends to happen in areas where fewer adults are present. Each school has its own "hot spots." These hot spots may include hallways, stairwells, locker rooms, restrooms, playgrounds, and cafeterias. And keep in mind, bullying can also happen right in the classroom setting, in front of the teacher. Students may pass a threatening note or give nasty, dirty looks without the teacher noticing.

.

The reality is bullying happens in many different ways and is instigated by both boys and girls. Relationships with our co-workers and bosses can really affect our lives! When they go well our lives are enriched. When they are difficult, we and our families can suffer.

• Maintain your Self qualities when you are under the gun: Stay Cool, Calm, Collective, Clarity, Connection, Compassion, Courage, Creativity, and Confidence

- Pay attention to them, and they may let you get back to your Self qualities and Self leadership.

Read on to find out how Internal Family Systems can help you at work.

Maybe your boss or co-worker:

Is unaware of your contributions Is uncaring about your feelings

Uses your services without thanks or acknowledgment

Insults you Is unappreciative

Steals credit Intimidates you

Changes plans without telling you

Doesn't apologize

Reacts defensively to feedback

Do you bounce between wanting to fight this person or leave the job?

Do you spend too much time seething, losing sleep over it, or feeling helpless?

Do you find yourself complaining to others and not to the one you're upset with?

If you've had these experiences you know how hard it is to deal with difficult co-workers or bullies at work. But there is something you can do.

Ten Principles for dealing with bullies & difficult people at work:

1. Don't try to win.

You won't win. Bullies and difficult people are often willing to fight dirty. You won't want to descend to their level. Trying to win weakens your communication <http://www.goodtherapy.org/therapy-for-communication-problems.html>. Instead of trying to win:

Try to communicate clearly

Stay calm

Speak in a way that you can respect yourself

Focus on maintaining your own calm, connection, confidence, and clarity

Judge the success of your communication by how clearly you express yourself, not by winning

Bullies will probably not admit their errors in front of you, but they may change their behavior.

2. Don't try to change the bully.

Bullies are not usually concerned about their behavior. You can waste a lot of energy trying to change bullies. Don't do it! If a person has been bullying others for months or even years forcing them to stop bullying is not going to work over night. Bring attention to their error must be first, showing them how alternative ways of voicing themselves in a positive way even when they don't get their way is another way, and lastly reversing the role of the bully to a protector of a bully may give the former bully a positive light on helping the weak, feeble, those that are preyed upon.

3. Confrontation is sometimes necessary.

You may need to stick up for yourself. It's not easy but if you prepare yourself ahead of time you can do it. Whether the confrontation is over shared credit, irritating co-worker habits, or to keep a project on track, sometimes you need to confront a coworker or a boss. The good news is that while confrontation is almost never your first choice, you can become better and more comfortable with necessary conflict. When you do confront, remember to:

Feel a sense of connection with the person you are confronting

Stay calm – Take Deep Breaths - Be clear

Be courageous - Avoid forcing; be patient about any change

5. Don't judge the person too quick.

When you judge another person you lose your power. State your beliefs and experiences clearly with NO judgment of the other person and simply bring them to the light of what they are doing. Judging the other person will only make them defensive & will provoke them to fight or rebel, simply because they are called on the carpet. If you don't judge, they don't have an opening to fight. Keep in mind to judge the action and not the person.

6. Be clear & specific about your experiences.

Use short, clear sentences and simple, unambiguous words. Let the other person know that you know they want control, but that "you don't have time for foolishness."

7. Talk mainly about yourself, your current experiences, and your preferences.

Avoid talking about the other person's behavior. That will usually get you a defensive, attacking response. Focus on your experiences – nobody can say you don't feel the way you do. It's hard to argue with someone when they are just saying how they feel about something.

Instead of saying: You are so unappreciative of my contributions.

Say: Like anybody, I want to be appreciated and acknowledged for what I do here. I don't hear much appreciation from you.

Instead of saying: You insult me all the time.

Say: I like to hear productive, direct feedback about my work. Insulting or demeaning comments don't help me and that's not the kind of working environment I want.

Emphasize preferences over demands. Saying what you prefer is very powerful. Demanding something can leave you powerless, because what will you do if you don't get your demands? Quit? If you aren't ready to quit, don't demand.

Instead of saying: I need you to acknowledge me for my contributions to the project.

Say: I prefer being acknowledged for my contributions.

8. Stay connected.

You may think that you should be cold to make a powerful statement. Or that connecting with the person means that you are condoning their behavior. Or maybe that if you connect you will be consumed by their negativity. None of this is true. You will be more powerful, have a bigger effect, and be better able to maintain your own positive energy if you feel connected to the person.

9. Be prepared if the response is not good.

Don't anticipate a good response. Nobody likes feedback, and bullies are no exception. Be ready for anything! Before you confront the person, think ahead about the bad responses you might get, and prepare yourself for each one. Are you going to collapse, get angry http://www.goodtherapy.org/therapy-for-anger.html , or give up if you don't get the response you want? Plan ahead to make a different response. The chapter on feedback in Bring Yourself to Love has a worksheet to help you with this.

10. Don't get caught in being too "nice."

You may think you have to be the nice person – the pleaser, the peacemaker, the well-liked person. Bullies may not respond to this. Ask yourself why you need to do this. Is it a habitual pattern? Did you have a volatile situation in your childhood so you felt you needed to be the calm, peaceful one? What are you trying to accomplish by being the nice one? You probably have good intentions, but this may not be the right situation for these intentions. See if you can talk yourself out of being nice, and instead be clear, direct, and aware of yourself and the responses you are getting.

11. If something inside you gets in the way of following these suggestions, be kind to yourself.

Does all this seem like a tall order? If you think you'll have difficulty with these suggestions, here's the best way to overcome them:

Acknowledge and appreciate what might get in the way.

You developed habits and patterns for a reason – they helped you grow up in your family and culture.

Be kind to these parts of you. They have good intentions.

Bully can produce mental health issues

Let's take a look at bullying. Bullying produces fear and fear produces stagnation, frustration & even total shut down.

I.   How you can defend yourself from a bully
II. The Mindset of a Bully
III. Why do they bully
IV. Who are their normal victims

How often does bullying occur?

"It is said that, every seven minutes, a child on an elementary playground is bullied."
(Pepler, Craig, & Roberts, 1998).

If these stats are as frequent as they are then truly the school staff should be aware of what's going and able to disarm the bullies, by telling them that this type of behavior will not be tolerated, right. Not exactly, the bully and the bullies must be educated on what bullying is and how to recognize it, effective ways to stop it, and simply bring more awareness to it in order that those that are around it may be willing to take a stand and confront it, thus in hopes to stop it.

Here is another alarming stat about bullying among the youth, which say that According to the American Medical Association, 3.7 million youths engage in bullying, and more than 3.2 million are victims of "moderate" or "serious" bullying each year (Cohn & Canter, 2003).

This book is more than just bringing awareness to this epidemic it's about arming the weak and the bystanders with

"MENTAL AND PSYCHOLOGICAL

BULLY PROOF TACTICS

FOR THE VICTIM"

The Solution

WIT4Life

WIT4LIFE

A POWERFUL SOLUTION TO BULLYING

Anger Management & Conflict Resolution

Made Easy for Children & Youth:

WIT4LIFE

"USE YOUR WIT4 LIFE"

A Life's Coach/ Parent/ Teacher/ Therapist/ Student Manual & Handbook to decrease Bullying & Agression

John W. Rhodes

Disclaimer: This anger management & conflict resolution technique is not a substitute for professional and legal help with anger and or conflicts. One should seek therapeutic and professional therapy to help with anger and conflicting situations, events. Only consistent and proper use of this anger management tool can be beneficial to the participant with proper counseling. The reader and participant of this program Anger Management & Conflict Resolution Made Easy for Children and Youth: WIT4LIFE, is asked to seek once again additional counsel, professional mental health assistance. This is not a fit all solution, if the participant who will be using these anger management and, neither should it be used along without therapeutic assistance.

SPECIAL THANKS

To Reba Johnson for your many hours of editing

the initial writings of this book. To my supportive wife Glenda and Son John Solomon who have been very patient during the many late hours I spent in front of the computer editing, re-writing and correcting errors.

TO THOSE WHO HAVE BEEN SUPPORTIVE AND ENCOURAGING me from the inception of WIT4LIFE to put it in a book form that others can use and apply to help kids, which is what this technique is all about.

Last, but not least, I thank God for the strength & his grace to carry out what he has gifted me to do.

TABLE OF CONTENTS

- Disclaimer: PLEASE READ BEFORE USING - WIT4LIFE
- INTRODUCTION
- WHAT MAKES WIT4LIFE DIFFERENT FROM OTHER A.M. & C.R. TECHNIQUES?
- WHY THE WORDS "PRESERVING HUMAN LIFE"?
- Youth Violence Statistics
- To the reader & user of this MANUAL & HAND BOOK
- What is Anger?
- What is Anger Management?
- What is Conflict Resolution?
- Goal
- Aim
- What's in a Name?
- Instructions before applying
- Before you begin
- Process of WIT4LIFE
- WIT4LIFE: Breakdown of W.I.T.T.T.T.
- Tools
- Affirmation Cards
- Classroom Poster

- Behavior Goal Chart
- Monitoring and Tracking
- Monitoring Tools
- Re-enforcement to use with WIT4LIFE
- Approach with participant
- Other resources
- Personal note from the author
- DISCLAIMER REMINDER

Introduction

Finally! An anger management technique and conflict resolution that children can relate to, hang on too, skateboard with, and share with peers, that's is "tight", "cool", what ever fly terms that our kids use today. I'm probably behind times when it comes to hip talking, "You Think", any way let me stop before the young ones start busting me out.

I have been driven to complete this due to the over whelming response from my fellow clinicians, therapist, teachers, school teachers, safe physical management teachers, family, friends and most of all parents of clients to write this book.

To see the change in my clients behavior over time is very rewarding and gratifying. Let me say that I count it a privilege for my clients to allow me the opportunity to share my life with them in a therapeutic way to help bring calm, balance and control in their lives. To all my clients I ever worked with I say to you, "THANK YOU VERY MUCH."

It's not often given where one is encouraged to use their creativity in the mental health field to impact others. The anger management skills I have acquired over the years are priceless to me and no text book can take the place of experience gathered over the years with my clients. I feel blessed with the opportunity to share with you only a snippet of the behavior techniques I have developed and created. Again, I say to you thank you for taking the time out to read, use and apply all that is written within these pages.

Thank you for purchasing a copy of this book, for it encourages me to write even more books. This has been a great journey. My hope is that others will be inspired to do the same with the hidden gifts and talents they have been endowed and blessed with.

THANK YOU.

WHAT MAKES WIT4LIFE DIFFERENT FROM OTHER…..?

WHAT MAKES WIT4LIFE: Anger Management Technique & Conflict Resolution different from all the rest of the anger management & conflict resolutions solutions?

We provide immediately quick, simple, innovative, memorable techniques that can be recalled by the child for immediately application. W4L also provides the adult/ parent a comprehensive, quick, simple effective guide that can be used to teach participants in a non- intimidating approach. **WIT4LIFE can be taught today, and learned & applied by the child/ youth starting today.** We use captivating techniques that get the attention of most of our participants immediately due to the innovative non- traditional ways of using anger management interventions. PLEASE USE THE TOOLS PROVIDED.

MENTAL NOTE: The instructor, teacher, parent, or anger management behavior coach should keep in mind to have fun with this concept and present it to the participant with excitement. Even if the participant is not excited at the moment just your enthusiasm alone has the tendency to inspire others, because that you are excited. Excitement breeds and enthusiasm increases application (desire to practice/do what was taught). Expect to be ready for your participants and don't expect them to be ready for you.

Presentation with passion and empathy is everything.

Let me first start off by saying that "there is nothing new under the sun", just different ways of teaching, learning and expressing our ideas. What I did was take that which have been used for centuries, by the ancients, therapist, psychologist, non-violent activist, anger management coaches, myself, etc. and made it applicable to the our times of contemporary development.

WHY THE WORDS PRESERVING HUMAN LIFE?

ANGER MANAGEMENT & CONFLICT RESOLUTION MADE EASY FOR CHILDREN AND YOUTH: WIT4LIFE, are wise & witty strategies put into the most simplistic and comprehensive form to help children and youth learn how to control emotions and preserving life, thus is why it is called WIT4LIFE.

Why do I use the words, "Preserving Life"?. When one doesn't learn to control their emotions and allow anger to take over, other people are hurt, offended and lives can even be lost due to violence. Violence & fatal deaths can be the end result of un-controlled anger & and senseless acts. Thus, if we can give a child anger management skills, plus help them understand the philosophy of non-violence, then our living is not in vain.

CONDITIONING OF THE MIND & SPIRIT

"Always aim at complete harmony of thought and word and deed. Always aim at purifying your thoughts and everything will be well." - Mohandas Gandhi

"A man who was completely innocent, offered himself as a sacrifice for the good of others, including his enemies, and became the ransom of the world. It was a perfect act."
Mohandas Gandhi

Youth Violence Stats

I shall allow no man to belittle my soul by making me hate him.
Booker T. Washington, American educator (1856-1915)

Statistics

- Among boys, 42% of high schoolers and 32% of middle schoolers believe it is okay to hit or threaten a person who makes them angry. One in five (20%) of the girls agrees. [Josephson Institute, 2006 Report Card on the Ethics of American Youth]

- An even higher percentage resorts to violence: 88% of all boys and over 76% of girls surveyed said they hit someone in the past 12 months because they were angry. [Josephson Institute, 2006 Report Card on the Ethics of American Youth

- In study after study, about 30-40 percent of boys and 15-30 percent of girls reports having committed a serious violent offense by age 17. [Youth and Violence: A Report of the Surgeon General, January 2001]

- In 2004, 5,292 young people ages 10 to 24 were murdered -- an average of 15 each day [Youth Violence Facts at a Glance, Summer 2007, U.S. Centers for Disease Control and Prevention (CDC)]

- Children in adult jails commit suicide eight times as often as their counterparts in juvenile facilities. In addition, children in adult facilities are five times more likely to be sexually assaulted, and twice as likely to be beaten by jail staff. [Children's Defense Fund, 1998]

- Among boys, 42% of high schoolers and 32% of middle schoolers believe it is okay to hit or threaten a person who makes them angry. One in five (20%) of the girls agrees. [Josephson Institute, 2006 Report Card on the Ethics of American Youth]

- On Bullying – An estimated 30% of 6th to 10th graders in the United States were either a bully, a target of bullying, or both(Nasel et at.2001) (CDC).

- Juveniles accounted for 16% of all violent crime arrests and 26% of all property crime arrest in 2007 (Puzzancera 2009)

- Less than 1% of all homicides and suicides among school-age youth occur on school grounds, on the way to or from school, or on the way to or from school-sponsored events (Anderson et al.2001)

- From 1999 to 2006, most school-associate homicides included gunshot wounds (65%), stabbing or cutting (27%), and beating (12%) (CDC 2008)

For more youth violence statistics visit:
www.cdc.gov/violenceprevention

TO THE READER AND USER OF THIS MANUAL & HAND BOOK

Are you looking for an anger management conflict tool or system that will help you make positive changes in your life, students, child or people you care about. When it comes to controlling anger and emotions I believe WIT4LIFE is one of the aides that can be used in addition to professional and legal anger management treatment. This is not a one fits all solution for anger control, but an additional resource to help in gaining authority over your emotions.

WIT4 Life is a cutting edge anger management technique/ strategy that can be effective at all age levels.

From time to time life can be cumbersome. We sometimes become distracted and need help to get back on track and to resolve issues. The natural tendency of some people is to respond defensively or impulsively when they feel threatened or when their space has been invaded. WIT4 Life is a broad based approach to early prevention to violence, bullying and type like conflicts. The conflict resolution technique in this handbook will provide a self-directed strategy to help individuals bring about or reach a desired behavior. WIT4 Life will help individuals manage their anger and resolve conflicts early. Most importantly, WIT4LIFE was written to serve as a tool to help reduce violence, aggression, identify anger triggers and to increase self worth and self esteem in children & youth while they learn these self controlling & emotion mastering principles. Once the student masters the technique, and the embedded strategies, they can be used for the rest of their life, in addition pass on to others for future use.

Disclaimer: This anger management technique when used and applied properly will help many individuals. The implementer must take in note the mental, comprehensive and emotion capability of the participant of the technique. It is not a fit all solution, neither should it take the place of the need for the participant to seek on going therapy from a certified or licensed and legal professional. We make no claims to guaranteed results from using this anger management and conflict resolution technique: WIT4LIFE model.

What is Anger?

"A soft answer turns away wrath: but grievous words stir up anger." - Proverbs

    Exactly, what is anger? An emotion that occurs when you feel your self-worth is violated, when our needs are not being met and when we feel like we are not being understood. We all get anger from time to time and often have a strong need to express that anger, like the other day when a car almost hit me by driving in my lane due to not paying attention, because he was busy talking on the cell phone. Of course, I wanted to give him a piece of my mind, but I decided to keep part of my mind and continue focusing on the thoughts I was enjoying, before the incident. Anger is not bad, it is when we allow anger to cause us to do something that could potentially put someone else life in danger, hurt someone else's feelings, or become disruptive in an organized setting. What is needed to control the emotion of anger is a self calming technique or way to organize the emotion of anger whereby it doesn't drastically effect others or ourselves, thus is where WIT4LIFE – Anger management & conflict resolution comes in.

What is Anger Management?

The term anger management commonly refers to a system of psychological therapeutic techniques and exercises by which one with excessive or uncontrollable anger can control or reduce the triggers, degrees, and effects of an angered emotional state. (Anger+Management*Wikipedia) (references)

Anger management **is really a non-violent strategy that has been use in for centuries   people just use different techniques and approaches they are comfortable with or taught.**

Anger is a feeling related to one's perception of having been offended/wronged and a tendency to undo that wrong doing by retaliation. R. Novaco recognized three modalities of anger: cognitive (appraisals), somatic-affective (tension and agitations) and behavioral (withdrawal and antagonism). Anger may have physical correlates such as increased heart rate, blood pressure, and levels of adrenaline and noradrenaline.[1]Some view anger as part of the fight or flight brain response to the perceived threat of harm.[2] Anger becomes the predominant feeling behaviorally, cognitively, and physiologically when a person makes the conscious choice to take action to immediately stop the threatening behavior of another outside force. (Wikipedia)

What is Conflict Resolution?

Conflict Resolution is defined by Wikipedia as **Conflict resolution** is a range of methods or eliminating sources of conflict. The term "conflict resolution" is sometimes used interchangeably with the term dispute resolution or alternative dispute resolution. Processes of conflict resolution generally include negotiation, mediation, and diplomacy.

One of the goals in teaching children & youth to control anger & resolve conflicts is to avoid disruption, disorder, violence, which is what anger leads to if not managed or controlled. Children must learn different ways of expressing their anger when feeling hopeless, abandoned or threatened. Anger comes out, in a physical expression, simply to function as a protective mechanism.

Dr. Leonard Ingram, of Chicago, IL, a personal mentor & friend of mine, who works with At Risk Youth in Boling, IL. , recently featured on ABC Morning News & BBC, founder of www.AngerMgmt.com, says that "one of the functions of anger is to protect oneself."

(photo From www.AngerMgmt.com)

He also says that knowing what "triggers the emotion of anger" can help one gain control of our anger before it gets out of hand. He says you must know the "self talk" that you are using. I personally, believe that this is also very important to controlling what you say that comes from what you are thinking. There is a powerful word from the bible that says, "Life and death are in the power of the tongue." Other words what you say or speak out of your mouth begins to take a form of itself once you speak it. So one must not only be careful what think, but also what they say as a result of the what they are thinking in the mind.

GOAL

      Our goal is to get the individual to solve the conflict early by simply applying the anger management and / conflict resolution skill WIT4LIFE. How does one gain control when tempers are flared, when one thing leads to another, either through child's play, or when an individual is trying to "save face"? W4L will help the student to resolve conflicts, control anger when their emotions are heightened, give the student a stronger philosophy non-confrontational strategies and personal power of being in control. The participant will also learn to recognize their emotions of anger, take control them using anger W4L technique & how it feels to respond positively to opposition. Emotional empowerment and learning to disarm another's hostile physical and verbal attacks against oneself is what this book is about. Now let us begin and "Use Your WIT4LIFE".

AIM

AIM OF WIT4LIFE

The aim o f WIT4LIFE is to teach the student/ child / participant simple steps they can use take to help manage their emotions in order to prevent out of control verbal, physical, or non-verbal non-compliant behaviors. There are times the child wished they hadn't said or done something that got them into deep trouble after the fact. Many kids display sorrow, or shame after the fact as well, and express they don't know why they did what they did. WIT4LIFE's aim is to give simple steps to redirect their actions that will result in a positive desired outcome. Thus, the participant will begin to feel good about themselves because they a choice to do the right thing in a challenging situation.

Before you start using this technique it is important to explain to the client what they are going to be learning and how it is going to benefit them.

*** Personal Philosophy. Using your WIT is like a great old proverb which says, "a soft answer turns away wrath. "

WHAT'S IN A NAME?

The first step is to have the facilitator whether it be parent/ teacher/ behavior coach/ mentor use WIT4LIFE to re-direct the participant immediately by calling their name. The first step is to **call their name**, this will get their attention. How can you re-direct someone who isn't aware that you are talking to them, and often when they are in a rage is difficult to re-direct them, thus calling their name makes them aware them aware that someone is paying attention to them as well. At this point you will say, for example, "Use Your WIT4LIFE (Jimmy/ Kelly)". Keep in mind that you have already explained to them the purpose of WIT4LIFE and that it will help them to control their anger & resolve personal conflicts, if and when ever needed.

Their name is that one thing that they consider personal and special so, don't over look the effort to call their name, before giving them instructions to follow.

INSTRUCTIONS BEFORE APPLYING WIT4 Life

(BEHAVIOR COACH / MENTOR/ PARENT/ TEACHER,ETC.)

Establishing a good rapport with the individual is the #1 key to implementing a successful intervention. After all, individuals tend to open up to people they know and trust, not to the the skill or technique they never met before and can't talk to. Get to know them, and walk in their world before you start giving this new behavior technique. EMPATHY leads the way to letting them know you truly care. They can feel it most of the time if you are just going through the motions or if you are truly concern about their development.

****Before You Begin...***

1. Explain the Process. What the child will learn.

2. Give examples. How it is done. .

3. Provide the Philosophy behind each Strategy (they are the steps W.I.T.4.Life).

The technique is the total package WIT4LIFE. .

4. Select the appropriate time. When the condition are feasible to use or apply the WIT4 Life Technique.

The implementer should be persistent, flexible, understanding, committed, willing to work with client on a daily basis, and patient. It takes time. Sometimes things get worse before they get better, but they will get better when you are hopeful and consistent teaching them the skills they need to succeed.

Make it fun, challenging and rewarding for the client. Constant re-enforcement is helpful in getting participant to buy into what you have to say.

Use a behavior chart and a visual WIT4 LIFE Poster/ Book Marker and visual and tangible re-enforcers.

The Importance of Tracking

Present a united front. Parents and professionals should know who's keeping track. Inform each other as much as possible on the behavior progress, month, weekly or daily if possible. This technique should be used as often as needed and as long as needed until the participant has established a firm knowledge, understanding and application.

"To know is not a mere tragedy but to know, and not put into action is."

PROCESS OF WIT4 Life

"Breaking It Down"

Implementers will begin showing each individual how to use WIT4Life by demonstrating a visual and or verbal cue. This must be pre-established. An example would be to put up three fingers (for W) four fingers (for the number 4) and an L demonstrated with the pointer finger and the thumb). With repeated trials, and considerable amount of time, {two months of practice on a daily basis} the client can recognize the antecedents and will hopefully start to self correct without cues. This includes teaching them to use a self affirming cue such as repeating to themselves, "Use my WIT4 Life, "Use My WIT", etc. (Positive Affirmation Cards/Poster). These STEPS helps to redirect and Enforce WIT4LIFE to control anger and avoid the conflicts.

WALK AWAY

- W – Walk Away. **The individual will simply walk away when they are confronted with a situation or conflict. How? By** removing oneself from the proximity, by taking 5 or more steps away. Why? This helps the person de-escalate and to place space between them and the other person. When? This should be done especially if one feels themselves about to confront, strike out, hit, curse, interrupt a class or group activity, etc.

As I have said once before the techniques that I have introduce to some, are being used and have been used for years. What I do is make the learning process, steps, simple for easy recall and application using acronyms and cognitive therapy strategies. Try going to http://www.anger-management-information.com and see some of the other reasons to use walking away as a strategy to manage your anger.

IGNORE NEGATIVE BEHAVIOR

- I –Ignore Negative Behavior/ Conflict/ Opposition. **The individual will simply _ignore_ the negative prompting or agitation of their peers when confronted.** *How? This can be done by having the student to turn their head in the opposite direction of the agitator or put their head down. This also can be done by pretending like you don't even hear the other person. However, they should be aware that this can also cause the provoker to become even more agitated so they must be on guard. Why? Because it is more important to take the high road, it will keep you out of trouble, it shows self-control, and it allows you to keep a mind of peace. You also earn the respect of the adults and peers, whether they tell you or not. Peers may call you a coward, call you names, or instigate. When? This is appropriate to do when someone does or says something directly to them to make you feel uncomfortable, or when they notice something being done to someone else.*

TAKE A DEEP BREATH

- **T1- *Take a Deep Breath.*** The individual will take a deep breath and blow out slowly before making any hasty decisions. How? Take a deep breath, hold it, blow out slowly and repeat this 3 or more times. Why? This allows oxygen to flow to your brain and it allows you regain or keep your composure. Taking a deep breath allow one time to think before acting upon their current emotion. In addition to this it will help you stop, and think before they act. When? One needs to take deep breaths when they feel their heart racing or beating faster than normal, or when other physiological changes occur.

TALK IT OUT IF POSSIBLE

- **T2- *Talk it out if possible*.** The individual will attempt to <u>talk the situation out</u> and <u>through with the peer or adult</u>. How? This is done in a calm and direct manner with the other person to let them know specifically how they are feeling or what they need. (Role play skills are important to do at this level of teaching) Why? <u>Talking it out</u> will allow one to communicate their feeling and concerns clearly, which will result in earlier resolution. This will teach them how to resolve a situation early. Again, WIT4 Life is a conflict resolution skill used to reduce or eliminate conflict all together if possible. This is what WIT4 Life is all about. When? This is done at the onset, before they are too upset to even reason it out with the other person.

TAKE A SELF TIME OUT

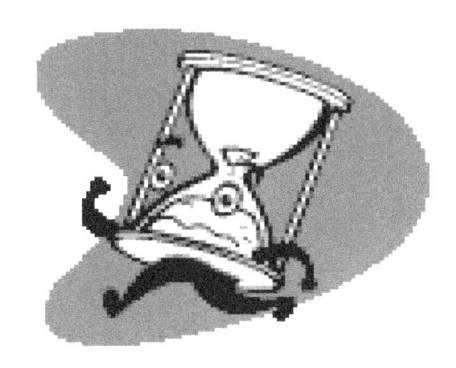

- T3- Stands for Take a Self Time Out. The individual will <u>take a self initiated moment to themselves</u>. How? By getting alone or <u>stepping away to a quiet place</u> where they can re-gather themselves and or calm down. This must be pre-determined and agreed upon by the adult/ teacher/ parent, etc. before this is done by the individual. Why? The importance of this is step back from the situation and to assess what is really happening. This also gives them an opportunity to think about what it is they need to do to avoid the conflict to even a greater measure when they arrive back into the class room/ setting where the opposing peer is located. When? It is important for the individual to move to another setting when they know they are getting agitated or if the other individual is trying to provoke them.

TELL SOMEONE/ AN ADULT

- T4- *Tell Someone*. *The individual will tell the teacher, an adult or parent. How? The individual will* tell someone *else in authoritative power, such as an adult or parent. They are to be specific once again and straight to the point. Why? To prevent oneself from getting into trouble. This will also allow them to cover themselves. By asking someone else for assistance they have a third party to help resolve the issue. When should they* tell someone? *When they do not feel comfortable addressing the situation alone.*

Please Use the following Tools/ Visual Aids when ever teaching WIT4LIFE to child/ youth:

- WIT4LIFE AFFIRMATION CARDS
- WIT4LIFE CLASS POSTER
- WIT4LIFE BEHAVIOR

GOAL CHART

WIT4LIFE AFFIRMATION CARDS

ANGER MANAGEMENT & CONFLICT RESOLUTION
for CHILDREN & YOUTH MADE EASY:
WIT4LIFE

WIT4LIFE

COPYRIGHT 2010 MCARES, INC. - JOHNWRHODES

USE YO' "WIT4LIFE"

- **W-** WALK AWAY
- **I -** IGNORE NEGATIVE BEHAVIOR
- **T-** TAKE A DEEP BREATH
- **T-** TALK IT OUT IF POSSIBLE
- **T-** TAKE A SELF TIME OUT
- **T-** TELL SOMEONE/ AN ADULT

WWW.WIT4LIFE.NET

ANGER MANAGEMENT & CONFLICT RESOLUTION
for CHILDREN & YOUTH MADE EASY:
WIT4LIFE

WIT4LIFE

COPYRIGHT 2010 MCARES, INC. - JOHNWRHODES

USE YO' "WIT4LIFE"

- **W-** WALK AWAY
- **I -** IGNORE NEGATIVE BEHAVIOR
- **T-** TAKE A DEEP BREATH
- **T-** TALK IT OUT IF POSSIBLE
- **T-** TAKE A SELF TIME OUT
- **T-** TELL SOMEONE/ AN ADULT

WWW.WIT4LIFE.NET

(Feel free to copy, laminate and give to students for quick recall)

WIT4LIFE CLASSROOM POSTER

ANGER MANAGEMENT & CONFLICT RESOLUTION
for CHILDREN & YOUTH MADE EASY:
WIT4LIFE

WIT4LIFE

COPYRIGHT 2010 MCARES, INC. - JOHNWRHODES

USE YO' "WIT4LIFE"

- **W -** WALK AWAY
- **I -** IGNORE NEGATIVE BEHAVIOR
- **T -** TAKE A DEEP BREATH
- **T -** TALK IT OUT IF POSSIBLE
- **T -** TAKE A SELF TIME OUT
- **T -** TELL SOMEONE/ AN ADULT

WWW.WIT4LIFE.NET

(Feel free to copy the above poster & POST IN YOUR CLASS ROOM/ OFFICE, etc.)

WIT4LIFE BEHAVIOR GOAL CHART

NAME_____ WEEK OF_____

WIT4LIFE STRATEGIES	MON.	TUES.	WED.	THUR.	FRI.	SAT
W-WALK AWAY						
I-IGNORE						
T-TAKE A DEEP BREATH						
T-TALK IT OUT						
T-TAKE A SELF TIME OUT						
T-TELL SOMEONE						

(COPY CHART AND USED DAILY TO MONITOR PROGRESS)

CHART 1 – WIT4LIFE Behavior Progress

www.wit4life.net

Monitoring and Tracking

It is so important to monitor and track the individual's progress in using WIT4 Life because you want to know how far the individual has come in applying the anger management the conflict resolution skill. In addition you want to know what is or is not working, in applying WIT4 Life. Monitoring on a daily and weekly basis will help you and the participant know how far along they are to reaching their behavior goal.

Goal: The goal would be to recognize origins of anger and develop alternatives to aggressive behavior, to also use these alternatives to release the emotional and/ or physical energy of anger.

Objectives: Will verbalize feelings of anger in a controlled, assertive way. Understand the concept of non-violence, plus utilize non-threatening behaviors/ anger management skill / techniques/ positive self-talk / relaxation techniques to cope with angry feelings.

A behavior treatment goal should be written out so that everyone is clear on the projected desired behavior.

To Parents and Professionals

Present a united front. Parents and professionals should know who is keeping track. Inform each other as much as possible on the progress, weekly or daily if possible. A Clear communication should be established between every individual who is actively involved in making sure that *WIT4 Life is carried out with the participant.*

Monitoring Tools:

Daily Progress of WIT4LIFE

<u>BEHAVIOR GOAL CHART</u>

1. WIT4 LIFE Daily Promptings – Affirmation Chart – done on a daily follow up basis to see what participant remembers to be ready when ever incidents occur.

Motivational Strategies

- <u>Praise the child</u> whenever they use portions of WIT4LIFE. This will increase their confidence to make good decisions and self-esteem at the same time.

- Use the prompting," Use Your WIT" as a secret code between the two of you. For example, "Jane maybe having a conflict in the classroom in front of others you will simply say to them, Jane use your WIT"

- One of the aims in using the prompting by saying, "Use Your WIT" to the student is try and reduce any probability of embarrassment when addressing the student/ client during a conflicting situation, while reminding them that they have a choice.

RE-ENFORCEMENTS TO USE WITH WIT4LIFE:

REWARDS – select these rewards with participant to let them know they have an active role in earning reward.

PRIVILEGES – same concept and approach as reward.

INCENTIVES – some will be immediate.

PRAISE – praise the participant immediately and find some type of reward you can give them.

These re-enforcements will work as a whole to bringing about a desire behavior or result.

The client/student should practice WIT4 Life on a daily basis with the parent, teacher, therapist, clinician or behavior coach on a consistent basis to get a desired result. This should be monitored on a daily, or weekly basis. Don't be frustrated if there are no immediate results, be patient with them and remember consistency is the key.

I have had times when my client didn't want to even use WIT4LIFE, but weeks after teaching them they reported back to me that they used there "WIT4LIFE" to resolve a conflict, or to prevent one from even happening. Then there was a time that the client and parent, reported back that next week the WIT4LIFE helped them. It may even take several months for the system to click in with the participant, just as long as you as the presenter stay consistent with the techniques is the main thing. You are not responsible if one uses WIT4LIFE, only teaching them the behavior modification system.

Reminder: Monitor Behavior

DAILY

WEEKLY

MONTHLY 'TIL LIFE

APPROACH WITH PARTICIPANT

(FOR THE TEACHER/PARENT/ THERAPIST/ ADULT, ETC.)

WIT4LIFE techniques has worked with many children and youth diagnosed with (ADHD) (ADD)(ODD), etc. The natural tendency of some of these clients is to respond defensively, impulsively when they feel threatened, challenged or when ever their space has been invaded, thus conflict may arise as a result. In addition to that they may feel a need to interrupt others conversations or conflict, even when it doesn't directly concern or affect them. Again, it's their attention deficit that prevents them from minding their own business. This is not a one fits all solution to helping a child to resolve conflicts, but is provided as anger management & conflict resolution tool.

Characteristics of (Attention Deficit Disorder) ADHD

Hyper, always busy, fidgety, blurting out in class, impatient, excessive talking, instigating peers or others conversations, leaves or roams around the class, acts socially inappropriate at times, low self-esteem, lack of self-control as described (*from DSM-IV TR, Manual of the American Psychiatric Association.*)

Why was "Use Your WIT4LIFE" formed?

Although I have good training and tools, plus behavior modification skills provided for me to give to my clients over the past 10 years as a clinical therapist, I realized that some of the techniques used with the children & clients I served just went over their heads. The kids were not able to retain the skills I shared with them. It was at this point WIT4LIFE behavior modification and cognitive therapy technique was created, while keeping intact cognitive therapy principles. After years of using these techniques and having success with my clients I decided to put these techniques in a book form so that parents, teachers, therapist and others can use to help their child, students, clients in resolving or avoiding conflicts.

By far *WIT4* has been the best cognitive behavior modification module I have created and used for conflict resolution and anger management, that has proven to be most effective with my clients.

It is simple and easy to remember. Using acronyms with the meaning behind it creates an imprint within the child's mind. Once WIT is spoken to the client as a reminder two things are happening, 1. They are being reminded to use the tool that they have, two the reward behind using it, and three, that they can be in control of their behavior, whether there response is in defense or offense to a particular situation. This skill will also help students with coping & decision making skills. Kids needs to know that there are programs, techniques, behavior strategies out there that can help them gain control of their emotions, resolve conflicts by themselves if needed.

Testimonials

"The WIT 4 LIFE Technique has been very beneficial with students who have difficulty controlling their anger. This technique gives students numerous options when feeling out of control." - Mary Freitag, Behavior Coach, William Wells Brown Elementary School

"WIT4LIFE was a technique used with several students in my Highly Structured Level classroom. This Anger Management technique proved to be very successful even with the students who struggled both with Behavior and with Cognitive skills. WIT4LIFE is a program/ strategy that can and will be successful over the course of a students' life time when they learn to use this technique."

- Melissa Kollros, SPED Teacher, Booker T. Washington Elem. Sch.

"This book is phenomenal! After reading it, I know that many kids and families will greatly benefit from it!"

Reba Johnson-Teacher of students in an Alternative setting Fayette County Public Schools in Kentucky.

Disclaimer: This anger management & conflict resolution technique is not a substitute for professional and legal help with anger and or conflicts. One should seek therapeutic and professional therapy to help with anger and conflicting situations, events. Only consistent and proper use of this anger management tool can be beneficial to the participant with proper counseling. The reader and participant of this program Anger Management & Conflict Resolution Made Easy for Children and Youth: WIT4LIFE, is asked to seek once again additional counsel, professional mental health assistance. This is not a fit all solution, neither should it be used along without therapeutic assistance

OTHER RESOURCE ITEMS

See website at
http://www.mcaresusa.com

- WIT4LIFE AFFIRMATION CLASS POSTER
- WIT4LIFE T-SHIRTS
- WIT4LIFE S.T.A.M.P. (SKATEBOARD TEACHING ANGER MANAGEMENT PORTAL)
- WIT4LIFE AFFIRMATION CARD
- WIT4LIFE BEHAVIOR GOAL CHART
- WIT4LIFE CLASS POSTER
- WIT4LIFE eBOOK
- Bully Proof Nation: Artistic & Character Building Music & Coaching

2 Set Curricullum CD

WIT4LIFE Blog:
http://wit4life.wordpress.com/

PERSONAL NOTE FROM AUTHOR

I was inspired to write this book because others have asked me to put this in a form whereby they can use these techniques with their student, child, etc. Therefore, I have stopped procrastinating and have eliminated fear of failure because I care too much for those whom this project can help greatly.

I created this cognitive behavior module as a way to help the kids I work with find a simple but yet manageable way of organizing their thoughts in a away to control their anger and resolve conflicts. Thus, from the over whelming success they were having and the request from teachers asking if I had something in print about wit4life they could use I was inspired to put this anger management technique in print.

ABOUT THE AUTHOR & LIFE COACH

PRESENTS

JW Rhodes
Author & Life Coach

'BULLY PROOF NATION'
ARTISTIC & CHARACTER BUILDING
MUSIC & COACHING

Coach JW Rhodes has worked as a clinical therapist with Severely Emotional Disturbed (SED) children and families for over 10 years. John has been married for over 14yrs. & father of four. He is also the founder of MCARESOFUSA – which stands for Multi-Cultural Arts Recreation & Educational Services, which is a artistic & character building curriculum program to help children & youth succeed in life through workshops, seminars, using Edu-tainment: Uni-cycling, skateboarding & original music, jazz, hip-hop, techno, etc. Topics ranging from Anti-Bullying, DREAMS, How to FOCUS, WIT4LIFE, Conflict Resolution, etc. He is originally from Chicago, Il and resides in Kentucky.

WIT4LIFE STAMP DVD: Skateboard Teaching Anger Management Portal

BULLY PROOF NATION ARTISTIC & CHARACTER BUILDING 2 SET CD MUSIC & COACHING CD also available on Amazon & iTune & **BULLY**

PROOF NATION usesArtistic & Character Building Music & Life Coaching. to teach children and youth how to succeed in life. This CD Bully Proof Nation is more than music. It educates while the listener engages. Bully Proof Nation CD includes Life Coach Music from Hip-Hop, Jazz, Spoken Word Flow, R&B Fill, Techno/House, Pop.

And Life Coaching to inspire and motivate positive actions of behavior in children & youth.

TWO CD PROGRAM SET:

CD1 - Life Coach Music

Listen here -->>> 1. Bully Proof Nation <<<--- ---

2. Got To Be Real

3. F.O.C.U.S.

4. WIT4Life

5. DREAMS in Your Hands

CD2 - Life Coaching with Coach Rhodes

1. Bully Proof Nation: "How to Arm yourself Against Bullying"

2. DREAMS in Your Hands: "How to Pursue Your Dreams"

All music was written & arranged and played

by JW Rhodes

http://mcaresusa.com

WIT4LIFE: Anger Management & Conflict Resolution for Children & Youth at *http://www.wit4life.net* & Blog: http://wit4life.wordpress.com – http://mcaresusa.com

Copyright 2010 MCARES, INC. & JOHN W RHODES

OTHER REFERENCES & RESOURCES

1. In Prevention for Teens | End to Cyber Bullying Organization (ETCB) at
http://www.endcyberbullying.org/prevention/prevention-for-teens/

2. Beware of Cyber Bullying - i-Safe
http://www.isafe.org/imgs/pdf/education/CyberBullying.pdf

3. WIT4LIFE: The Anger Management & Conflict Resolution Technique for children & youth by Jw Rhodes

4.

5. Bully by Lee Hirch & Cynthia Lowen with Dina Santorelli

6. I-Safe.org

7. How to talk to your kids about school violence by Dr. Ken Druck

8. It's Time to Take A Stand by Lee Hirch & Cynthia Lowen

9. Bullying Prevention & intervention by Cindy Miller, LCSW, & Cynthia Lowen
10. Little Girls Can Be Mean: Four Steps to Bully –Proof Girls in the Early Grades by Michelle Anthony, M.A., PH.d & Reyna Lindert, PH.D

11. The Bully, the Bullied, and the Bystander by Barbara Coloroso

COPYRIGHT 2014 jwrhodes & mcaresofusa

Made in United States
Orlando, FL
10 June 2024